"1988"

Happy Birthday Jim

Love,
The Christensens

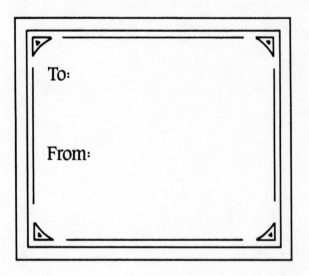

To:

From:

TABLE
GRACES

PRAYERS OF THANKS

Edited by Nick Beilenson

Illustrated by Michael McCurdy

PETER PAUPER PRESS, INC.
WHITE PLAINS • NEW YORK

Introduction

Table graces are prayers of thanks to God offered at the beginning of a meal. A simple grace such as "Lord, we thank Thee for the food we are about to receive. Amen" is sufficient.

However, a grace can also be longer, more poetic or spiritual, and more thought-provoking. In any event, saying different graces at breakfast or dinner, at various holidays and times of year, or in response to a minister's recent sermon or the news of the day enhances the spiritual and intellectual content of the experience.

Table graces bring a family together, keep us in touch with God and help us to remember our fellow men and women in need. Many people link hands as a physical symbol of the link between family and friends and between those at the table and all of God's children on earth.

Whatever the words of praise that we utter, God will hear our voices and understand our meaning. As an unknown poet once said:

> "Lord of the Universe, I am a simple man, an ignorant man. Oh, how I wish I had the words to fashion beautiful prayers to praise Thee! But alas, I cannot find these words. So listen to me, O God, as I recite the letters of the alphabet. You know what I think and how I feel. Take these letters of the alphabet and You form the words that express the yearning, the love for Thee that is in my heart."

More than a quarter of the graces in this book were compiled or composed twenty years ago by Paul Simpson McElroy, a contemporary religious thinker, and this book is dedicated to him. New graces, especially those with modern themes, were composed for this edition by Evelyn L. Beilenson and the editor. And the reader will find to his or her delight many familiar traditional graces, as well as adaptations of a number of well-known graces.

N.B.

Table Graces

DEAR LORD, we thank you for the blessings of friends and family here around your table. We ask that you make us all truly mindful of your gifts and help us to share them with others. Amen.

Kent F. Warner

✠

DEAR LORD, we thank Thee for the food we are about to receive, for the nourishment of our bodies. For Christ our Redeemer's sake. Amen.

✠

ALMIGHTY and gracious Father of men, who openest Thy hand and fillest the earth with good, and hast provided Thy children sufficient to satisfy all our needs; teach us to render back to Thee Thy due thanksgiving, not only in words, but also in the manner of our living. Amen.

7

FOR FOOD and drink and happy days,
Accept our gratitude and praise;
In serving others, Lord, may we
Repay in part our debt to Thee.

✠

GIVE ME a good digestion, Lord,
And also something to digest;
Give me a healthy body, Lord,
With sense to keep it at its best.

Found in Chester Cathedral, England

✠

YOU ARE BLESSED, Lord our God, King
of the Universe, who sustains the whole
world with goodness, graciousness, kindness and mercy. You provide food to all
living things. By your great goodness,
this world has provided and will in the
future provide food for all, so long as we
eat for the sake of your great Name.
There is enough food to feed us and
means to sustain us all, if only we would
eat to do good for those whom you have
created in your image. You are blessed,
Lord, who sustains all with food. Amen.

O LORD JESUS CHRIST, Thou Good Shepherd of the sheep, who came to seek the lost, and to gather them into Thy fold, have compassion upon those who have wandered from Thee; feed those who hunger, cause the weary to lie down in Thy pastures, bind up those who are broken in heart, and strengthen those who are weak, that we, relying on Thy care and being comforted by Thy love, may abide in Thy guidance to our lives' end. Amen.

THE EARTH is the Lord's and the fullness thereof. We praise Thy holy name that out of Thy plenty Thou hast so well remembered our necessities. Amen.

O LORD, Thou didst create the earth for man, and gave him the fruits of the earth and of the flocks and herds for his support, and hast said that our food is to be sanctified by prayer. Sanctify this food to us, and us to Thy service for Jesus' sake. Amen.

THOU ART GREAT and Thou art good,
And we thank Thee for this food;
By Thy hands will we be fed,
Give us, Lord, our daily bread. Amen.

LORD JESUS, be our Holy Guest,
Our morning joy, our evening rest,
And with our daily bread impart
Thy love and peace to every heart.
Amen.

THE EYES of all look hopefully to you, O
Lord. And you give them their food in
due season. You open your hand and fill
every living creature with blessing.

✠

O FATHER CREATOR, We ask this blessing
upon our food
And we ask for all your peoples
The growth of loving hearts
And the happy life of peace and harmony.
Arapaho Ceremonial Prayer

FOR SERVICE CLUB LUNCHEONS:

HEAVENLY FATHER, we thank you for the blessings of this day and the opportunity to be together at this table in fun and fellowship. Just as your Word and many promises nourish and strengthen our souls, may these gifts of food nourish and strengthen us in our particular places of work, where you have called us, so that we may always be of service to you through our neighbors and those in need. Amen.

Frederick J. Schumacher

✠

O GOD, our heavenly Father, who hast promised to provide, not for our every whim or wish, but for our every need, we thank Thee for these mercies. Grant unto us a due sense of appreciation, for those whose hearts and hands have wrought for us. Help us to share with others, that all Thy children may be strong in body, mind and spirit. Sanctify our fellowship by Thy presence; and may Thy blessing abide in our hearts.

Charles D. Brodhead

THE LORD my pasture shall prepare,
And feed me with a shepherd's care;
His presence shall my wants supply,
And guard me with a watchful eye.

Joseph Addison

OH, LORD bring all the
Ingredients of my life together,
And make me into the miracle
You want me to be.

DEAR LORD we thank you for your love
that we feel in our lives. We ask that you
help us to share this love with our co-
workers and friends.

DEAR LORD, we thank you for the bounty
of this, your table. And, as we accept
your gifts, help us to be accepting of others.

Kent F. Warner

12

LEADER: GOD is the Creator, the Master of nature.

All: God causes the tree to bear fruit and the earth to yield bread.

Leader: From God comes the wisdom by which we plant and harvest in abundance.

All: From God comes the energy hidden in the tiny seed and the mysterious chemistry of growth.

Leader: From God also comes the desire to share what we have with the hungry.

All: We together give thanks for the good earth and the blessing of food.

Graces from the Past

BE PRESENT at our table, Lord,
Be here and everywhere adored.
Thy creatures bless, and grant that we
May feast in paradise with Thee.

John Wesley

✠

MAN SHALL NOT live by bread alone, but
by every word that proceedeth out of the
mouth of God. (Matt. 4:4)

✠

O TASTE and see that the Lord is good:
blessd is the man that trusteth in Him.
(Ps. 34:8)

✠

MAY THE BLESSING of God rest upon you,
May his peace abide with you.
May his presence illuminate your heart
Now and forever more.

The Sufi Blessing

15

WE BEING many are one bread, and one body; for we are all partakers of that one bread. Whether therefore ye eat, or drink, or whatsoever ye do, do all to the glory of God. (I Cor. 10:17, 31)

✠

Benedic, Domine, nos et haec tua dona quae de tua largitate sumus sumpturi (per Christum Dominum nostrum). Amen. (Bless us O Lord and these Thy gifts which we are about to receive from Thy bounty through Christ our Lord. Amen.)

✠

GOD IS great and God is good,
And we thank Him for this food.
By His hand must all be fed;
Give us, Lord, our daily bread.
                              The Hampton Grace

✠

GIVE US grateful hearts, our Father, for all Thy mercies, and make us mindful of the needs of others.
                        Book of Common Prayer

WHAT GOD gives, and what we take,
'Tis a gift for Christ His sake:
Be the meal of beans and pease,
God be thank'd for those and these:
Have we flesh, or have we fish,
All are fragments from His dish.

Robert Herrick

PRAISED BE THOU, O God, who dost
make the day bright with Thy sunshine,
and the night with the beams of heavenly
fires. Listen now to my prayers; watch
over me with Thy power; give me grace
to pass all the days of my life blamelessly,
free from sin and terror. For with Thee
is mercy and plenteous redemption, O
Lord, my God.

Liturgy of Greek Church

PRAISE GOD from whom all blessings flow;
Praise Him, all creatures here below.
Praise Him above, ye heavenly host:
Praise Father, Son, and Holy Ghost.

The Doxology

OUR FATHER, we thank Thee that—

Back of the loaf is the snowy flour,
And back of the flour is the mill,
And back of the mill is the wheat and
the shower,
And the sun and the Father's will.

✠

THANKS be to Thee, my Lord Jesus Christ,
For all the benefits Thou hast given me,
For all the pains and insults Thou hast
borne for me.
O most merciful Redeemer, Friend, and
Brother,
May I know Thee more clearly,
May I love Thee more dearly,
May I follow Thee more nearly. Amen.

Twelfth Century Prayer

✠

FOR EACH new morning with its light . . .
For rest and shelter of the night,
For health and food, for love and friends,
For everything Thy goodness sends.

Ralph Waldo Emerson

OUR FATHER, by whose hand we are fed,
we bless Thee for this living bread.
Amen.

✠

SOME HAE meat and canna eat,
And some would eat that want it;
But we hae meat, and we can eat,
Sae let the Lord be thankit.

Robert Burns

✠

BE PRESENT at our table, Lord;
Be here and everywhere adored.
Thy children bless, and grant that we
May feast in fellowship with Thee.

Isaac Watts

✠

THEE LET us taste, nor toil below
For perishable meat;
The manna of Thy love bestow,
Give us Thy flesh to eat.

Charles Wesley (Grace Before Meat)

NOW THANK we all our God,
With heart and hand and voices
Who wondrous things hath done,
In whom His world rejoices.

Catherine Winkworth

✠

ALL good things around us
Are sent from heaven above;
We thank the Lord, O thank the Lord,
For all His love.

Matthias Claudius

✠

WE THANK THEE, O Lord our God, for
all Thy goodness. Thou hast shielded,
rescued, helped, and guided us all the
days of our lives, and brought us unto
this hour. Grant in Thy goodness that we
may spend this day without sin, in joy
and reverence of Thee. Drive away from
us all envy, all fear. Bestow upon us what
is good and meet. And lead us not into
temptation, but deliver us from evil.

Unknown

IT IS very nice to think
The world is full of meat and drink
With little children saying Grace
In every Christian kind of place.

Robert Louis Stevenson

THE BLESSING of God rest upon all those
who have been kind to us, have cared for
us, have worked for us, have served us,
and have shared our bread at this table.
Our merciful God, reward all of them in
your own way, for yours is the glory and
the honor forever.

St. Cyril of Alexandria

Graces for Children and Youth

LORD, we thank Thee for our food;
Make it help us as it should.
Make us strong to work and play,
   day by day.
Thou art very kind and good—
Lord, we thank Thee for our food.

THANK you, God,
For food so good,
Lord help us do
The things we should.

DEAR GOD, again I bow my head,
And thank Thee for my daily bread.

I thank Thee, God, again today
That I am well, that I can play.

Thank Thee for friends so good to me;
Help me a good, kind friend to be.

Norman S. Schlichter

GOD IN ME and God in you
There lies all the good we do.
We thank you, Lord, that this is so;
We thank you that we live and grow.

O GOD, our Father, who giveth food for
the body and truth for the mind; so en-
lighten and nourish us that we may grow
wise and strong to do Thy will.

THANK Thee, Lord, for loving me.
Help me now to be
Happy and helpful every day
For all you give to me.

OUR GRACIOUS heavenly Father, we thank
Thee for food:
    —for food for our bodies,
    —for food for our minds,
    —for food for our spirits,
Help us to appreciate Thy gifts and use
them in Thy service.

Bless us, Jesus, in our home;
And bless kids across the sea.
Please send needed food and drink
To children everywhere—and me.

✠

Thank you, God, for milk and bread
And other things so good.
Thank you, God, for those who help
To grow and cook our food.

✠

O the Lord is good to me,
And so I thank the Lord,
For giving me the things I need:
The sun, the rain, and the appleseed.
The Lord is good to me.

Attributed to Johnny Appleseed

✠

Thank you for the food we eat;
Thank you for the friends we meet;
Thank you for our work and play:
Thank you, God, for a happy day.

O GIVE thanks, O give thanks,
O give thanks unto the Lord,
For He is gracious and His mercy endur-
eth forever. (A round)

FOR HEALTH and strength
And daily bread
We praise Thy name, O Lord. (A round)

GOD has created a new day,
Silver and green and gold.
Live that the evening may find us
Worthy His gifts to hold.

Lord bless not only meat and drink,
But what we do and what we think.
So that in all our work and play,
We may grow better every day.

For God's stately pine trees,
For the love which brought us here,
Make us thankful, Lord, and loyal
To our camp (school) and comrades dear.

For FRUIT and milk
For bread and meat,
For all this food
So good to eat—
We thank you, God. Amen.

✛

THANK YOU, O God, so good,
For today's bread.
Thank you for watching over us,
Thank you for your love.

✛

I'D BE as impolite a child
As impolite could be,
To eat and quite forget to say
A thank you, Lord, to Thee.

✛

He gave us eyes to see them,
And lips that we might tell,
How great is God Almighty,
Who has made all things well. Amen.
Cecil Francis Alexander

27

We thank thee, Lord, for happy hearts,
For rain and sunny weather.
We thank Thee, Lord, for this our food,
And that today we are together.

✠

For bright lights and warm fires,
  We thank Thee, O God;
For good food and the clothes we wear,
  We thank Thee, O God;
For the love and care of mother and father,
  We thank Thee, O God;
For friends who come to be our guests,
  We thank Thee, O God;
For all things you have given us to enjoy,
  We thank Thee, O God;
For true happiness which comes when
we share,
  We thank Thee, O God.

✠

All things bright and beautiful.
All creatures great and small,
All things wise and wonderful:
The Lord God made them all.

HERE a little child I stand
Heaving up my either hand;
Cold as paddocks though they be,
Here I lift them up to Thee,
For a benison to fall
On our meat and on us all.

Robert Herrick

✠

OUR FATHER, we are grateful for this
family, who hand in hand form one un-
broken circle. Help us to do Thy will, as
caring individuals and as a loving family.
Amen.

✠

THANK YOU for the world so sweet,
Thank you for the food we eat,
Thank you for the birds that sing.
Thank you, God, for everything.
Amen.

E. Rutter Leatham

29

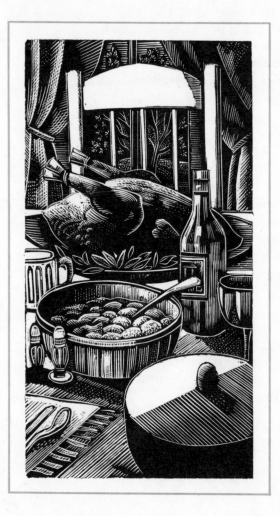

Graces for Holidays and Special Occasions

NEW YEAR'S DAY

As we gather around the festive board this beautiful New Year's Day, we thank Thee dear Lord for Thy goodness to us, and pray God the hungry everywhere may be fed. Be with us during this day, guide and keep us, we ask in His name. Amen.

WASHINGTON'S BIRTHDAY

Thou hast dealt kindly with us, Heavenly Father, in giving the grace of comfort and freedom. We rejoice in the privilege of a nation under a constitution and laws. We give thanks for our heroes and presidents. All this we acknowledge again unto Thee with thanksgiving. Amen.

ASH WEDNESDAY

O GOD, we think of the sins we have committed, and we repent and ask Thy forgiveness. We rely on Thy everlasting mercy. In the good food and drink that are placed before us, we look for your strength to preserve us. Amen.

PALM SUNDAY

ON THIS HOLY DAY we meditate on our Saviour, the Prince of Peace, whom you have sent into this world to redeem us from sin. Inspire us to accept Him as our Lord, and we say with gratitude—Amen.

GOOD FRIDAY

LORD, we ask you to bless our food on this day which commemorates our crucified Lord. We are with Him as He carries His cross to Calvary Mount. May we accept Christ and this food with humility and with love. Amen.

EASTER

THIS DAY, O Christ, we celebrate Thy victory over death. Bring to us new life of body through this nourishment, and new life of soul by Thy presence with us now and help us to say with Thy servant of old: "Thanks be to God which giveth us the victory through Jesus Christ our Lord." Amen.

✠

AT THIS EASTER sunrise, we are inspired by the tidings of eternal life through the risen Christ, Thy only son. With gratitude we ask blessing for this food now set before us, in Jesus' name. Amen.

MOTHER'S DAY

TODAY we give special thanks to our mothers, whether here on earth or departed, who have loved us and guided us from infancy to maturity. Amen.

MEMORIAL DAY

O GOD, we thank Thee that Thou hast
preserved us a nation with liberty and
justice. Help us this day to honor the
men who fought and died for our
Union. We salute with gratitude the living veterans of World Wars I and II, Ko-
rea and Vietnam. May we realize how
near the spirit of patriotism is to Thine
own great Heart, and may we serve Thee
the better for the memories of today.
Amen.

✠

LORD, we remember those brave Ameri-
cans who gave their lives to protect our
country's physical integrity and its ways
of democracy and freedom. They died so
that we could live in peace and tranquili-
ty. We give thanks that we can today
come together at this table with abun-
dant food, in harmony and in peace.
Amen.

FATHER'S DAY

On this special day we remember what is true all year long, that our fathers through love and pride have helped us to become responsible and loving human beings. We are the better because of our fathers' guiding examples. Amen.

INDEPENDENCE DAY

We ask Thy blessing today upon this glorious Republic. Shield her from error, guard her from corruption, make of her a nation after Thine own heart. For the liberty whose birthday we celebrate to-day, we give Thee gracious thanks, especially for the liberty of serving Thee according as Thou dost give us wisdom. Vouchsafe Thy continued providence over us, and eventually may we be gathered at Thy right hand in glory. Amen.

LABOR DAY

As we ask Thy blessing upon our home today, we ask too that Thou wilt graciously bless the homes of all those who live by the sweat of their brow. Give us the health to labor on, and grace to be proud of labor, remembering the example of our Lord, and his word of commendation that the laborer is worthy of his hire. Continue with us this day and evermore. Amen.

THANKSGIVING DAY

Once more we come, Lord, to this day of special thanksgiving. Our thoughts are turned backward, to the Pilgrims and Indians and also to this past year. The days have rolled into the seasons, the seasons into the year. Each day has been crowded with Thee. Each season has brought forth new proofs of Thy loving forethought. May we this day pledge Thee our gratitude anew. Continue, we pray Thee, to surround us with Thy care, in Jesus' name. Amen.

CHRISTMAS MORNING

WE THANK Thee for the blessings received during the days that are gone, and ask Thy Divine blessing upon this food this Holy Christmas morning, for Jesus' sake. Amen.

CHRISTMAS EVENING

WE THANK Thee for this day's feast, instituted by the Birth of Thy Holy Son. Bless us and guide us through all time, we ask for Jesus' sake. Amen.

NEW YEAR'S EVE

TONIGHT we celebrate that we have lived yet another year wrapped in Thy warm embrace. Throughout this past year, Thy love has sustained us. We ask that, in the year to come, Thou guide us along the straight and narrow path to Thy love. Amen.

Morning and Evening Graces

FOR THIS NEW morning and its light, For rest and shelter of the night, For health and food, for love and friends, For every gift His goodness sends, I thank Thee, gracious Lord. Amen.

Unknown

✠

FATHER for this morning
   (noonday, evening) meal
We would speak the praise we feel.
Health and strength we ask of Thee,
Help us, Lord, to faithful be.

✠

IT IS A GOOD thing to give thanks unto the Lord and to sing praises unto Thy name, O Most High, to show forth Thy loving kindness in the morning and Thy faithfulness every night. Amen.

O LORD, all creatures wait upon Thee that they may receive their good. Thou openest Thy hand, and they are filled with good. Help us to remember always that we are dependent upon Thee and with thankfulness partake of the food before us.

PRAISED be Thou
O Lord our God,
Ruler of the world,
Who causes the earth to yield food for all.

O GOD, we thank Thee for this food: as we live by Thy bounty, may we live continually to Thy praise.

✠

LORD, PLACE Thy blessing upon us as we prepare to receive this food. We thank Thee for new strength, in Jesus' name. Amen.

OUR HEAVENLY Father, we thank Thee for this food and for the fellowship of this table. We pray that this food may strengthen us physically and this fellowship may enrich us spiritually that we may the better do Thy will.

OUR FATHER, we give thanks to Thee for this food, and we also remember in gratitude the men and women, near and far, whose labors have made this meat possible. Grant that they may enjoy the fruit of their labor without want, and that they may be bound with us in a fellowship of thankful hearts.

MOST MIGHTY LORD and merciful Father, we yield Thee hearty thanks for our bodily sustenance, requiring also, most entirely, Thy gracious goodness, so to feed us with the food of Thy heavenly grace that we may worthily glorify Thy holy name in this life, and after be made partakers of the life everlasting.

41

OUR GRACIOUS Father, we thank Thee
for the tree which brings forth fruit in
season, for ripening grain, for meat that
strengthens the heart of man. May we
not be unmindful of the love which
planned all things well for Thy children.

✠

PRAISE TO GOD, immortal praise,
For the love that crowns our days;
Bounteous source of every joy!
Let Thy praise our tongues employ;
All to Thee, our God, we owe,
Source whence all our blessings flow.

✠

WE THANK Thee, our heavenly Father,
for Thy care over us and pray that Thou
wilt bless this food to our use.

✠

FATHER in heaven, sustain our bodies
with this food, our hearts with true
friendship, and our souls with Thy truth.

42

BLESS US, O Lord, and these Thy gifts, which we are about to receive from Thy bounty.

✠

THANKS BE to Thee, O Lord, for these and all the blessings so generously provided.

✠

BLESSED IS GOD in all His gifts; and holy in all His works. Our help is in the name of the Lord, who hath made both heaven and earth. Blessed be the name of our Lord, from henceforth, world without end.

✠

FOR DAILY BREAD, for all things good,
For life and health, for this our food,
For each good gift Thy grace imparts,
We thank Thee, Lord, with humble hearts.

Clifford Wesley Collins

QUIETLY, LORD, Thy creatures raise their eyes to Thee, and Thou grantest them in due time their nourishment, ready to open Thy hand and fill with Thy blessing all that lives. Blessed be the name of the Lord.

ALMIGHTY Giver of Good, we thank Thee for Thy lovingkindness to us. Thou openest Thy hand, and we are fed. Be at this table, we pray Thee, and bless our gathering together.

FOR HEALTH, and strength, and daily food, We praise Thy name, O Lord.

✠

ACCEPT, O Father, our humble thanks for this our daily bread; and as it adds strength to our mortal bodies, may it give us power to render better service to Thee.

No ORDINARY meat—a sacrament—
   awaits us
On our daily spread,
For men are risking lives on sea and land
That we may dwell in safety and be fed.

As told to Cecil Hunt

✠

O GOD, make us able
For all that's on the table! Amen

Eire

✠

WE BLESS Thee, O God, for this food
which betokens Thy continued care over
us; we acknowledge this gift, and Thy
love which prompts it, and pray for fi-
delity to use our strength in doing Thy
good pleasure.

✠

THIS FOOD, which Thou hast already
blessed in the giving, do Thou further
bless in our partaking, that it may re-
dound to Thy glory. Amen.

45

WE THANK Thee, God, for milk and
bread
   And all our daily food;
These gifts remind us day by day,
   Our Father, Thou art good.

Herman J. Sweet

FATHER, we thank Thee for this food,
For all the blessings Thou dost give;
Strengthen our bodies and our souls,
And let us for Thy service live.

O GOD, who hast given us much, we lift
our hearts to Thee in gratitude, and
pray that Thou wilt make us quick to
share the best we have with those who
are in need.

O GOD, bless our home, our family,
friends and neighbors, and give us
thankful hearts for all Thy mercies.

OUR FATHER, we bless Thee for this food
and for all expressions of Thy goodness
to us. Give us grace ever to do Thy will.

✠

BLESSED art Thou, King of the Universe,
who bringest forth food from the earth.

✠

OUR FATHER, let the spirit of gratitude
so prevail in our hearts that we may
manifest Thy spirit in our lives.

W.B. Slack

✠

FOR THIS our daily bread, and for every
good gift which cometh down from
Thee, we bless Thy holy name.

✠

GRACIOUS FATHER, we give thanks to
Thee for the gifts we have enjoyed
through Thy bountiful goodness.

47

SANCTIFY, O Lord, we beseech Thee, this
food to our use, and us to Thy service,
and make us truly thankful for all these
mercies.

✠

WITH HEART as well as lips, dear God,
We thank you for this food;
For countless blessings too,
We offer gratitude.

✠

GRACIOUS Giver of all good,
Thee we thank for rest and food.
Grant that all we do or say
In Thy service be this day.

✠

I THANK Thee, Lord, that Thou hast kept
    The best in store;
We have enough, yet not too much
    To long for more;
A yearning for a deeper peace,
    Not known before.

Adelaide Anne Proctor

AT THIS TABLE, Lord, we ask
 That Thou wilt be our guest.
We thank Thee, Father, for this food,
 And may we all be blest.

WE'RE THANKFUL for the many things
Our heavenly Father sends:
For love and faith and strength and health,
For home and food and friends.

GIVE US grateful hearts, our Father, for
all Thy mercies, and make us mindful of
the needs of others.

FOR THESE and all His blessings may
God's holy name be praised.

BLESS, O Lord, these gifts to our use and
ourselves to Thy service.

LORD, Thou hast not need of our thanks, but we have daily need to remind ourselves of our obligation unto Thee. For all Thy mercies make us ever truly grateful.

✠

TO GOD who gives us daily bread
A thankful song we raise,
And pray that He who sends us food
Will fill our hearts with praise.

Mary Rumsey

✠

MAY GOD bless what His bounty hath provided.

✠

FOR WHAT we are about to receive, O Lord, make us truly grateful. Amen.

✠

TRANSFORM this food into life, O God, and transform that life into useful service of Thee. Amen.

LORD, gratitude we offer all who labor
that we may be fed; O dignify our toil
for them, Bring kinship through our daily bread.

Olive Haskins

✠

HEAVENLY FATHER, be our Guest;
  Our morning joy, our evening rest;
And with our daily bread impart
  Thy love and peace to every heart.

✠

LORD, make us truly grateful for the
blessings of this day, and keep us Thine
evermore.

✠

THOU hast given so much to us, give one
thing more: a grateful heart.

✠

BENEDICTUS benedicat. Amen. (May the
Blessed One bless.)

WE THANK Thee, Lord, that however hopeless our work may seem, however dark the night around us, however meagre the response to Thy Spirit, still Thou hast ordained for us a hope.

We Thank Thee that we can never despair because we know, past all doubting, that here and there in this world Thy kingdom has already come, Thy will has already begun to rule.

We Thank Thee that here and there are homes made beautiful by Thy presence, lives lived purely and faithfully for Thee, children and child-like souls whose clear and simple trust brings Thee Thyself down amongst men.

J.S. Howland

DEAR LORD we thank you for all the material and spiritual blessings that you shower on us. Help us to share all that we have with those who are less fortunate.

Kent F. Warner

GIVE US Lord, a bit o' sun,
A bit o' work and a bit o' fun;
Give us all in the struggle and sputter
Our daily bread and a bit o' butter.

On the wall of an old inn, Lancaster, England

✠

THANKS BE to Thee, O God, for the order and constancy of nature, summer and winter, seedtime and harvest, and the loveliness of each season in its turn; for a well ordered community, wise government and just laws; for education and the joys of the mind through letters, art and science; for the work we have to do, for strength to do it; for whatever of good there has been in our past lives; and for the hopes and aspirations that lead us on toward better things; for the discipline of life through which we are brought nearer to the common life of men; and for our high calling as servants on earth of Thy Kingdom; we give Thee thanks.

John Hunter

WE THANK Thee, heavenly Father,
  For every earthly good.
For life, for health, for shelter,
  And for our daily food.

✠

GOD who givest mouths for meat,
And today hast blessed our board,
Give us appetite to eat
To the glory of the Lord.

✠

WE THANK YOU, Father, for this food,
for the nourishment of our bodies. May
we be as faithful in serving you as you
are in providing for our daily bread.

✠

HEAVENLY FATHER, Thou hast given us
our daily bread. Out of our abundance
may we remember those of Thy children
who cry aloud to Thee for bread—but
have it not.

To God, who gives us daily bread
  A thankful song we raise,
And pray that He who sends us food
  May fill our hearts with praise.

Let Thy peace and blessing descend
upon us as we take of Thy bounty. Fill
our hearts with praise toward Thee and
love toward our fellowmen.

God, bless this food to our use, and
bless our lives to Thy service, and make
us in our blessings ever mindful of the
needs of others.

O God, our Father, be Thou the Unseen
Guest at our table, and fill our hearts
with Thy love.

Lord, help us to receive all good things as from Thy hand, and to use them to Thy praise.

✠

O Lord, how can we thank Thee for the continued mercies received at Thy hands. Each day we have cause to be profoundly grateful unto Thee. Accept our thanks, O Lord, for the great mercies Thou art constantly showing us, and help us to live a good and useful life and to be ever grateful for Thy mercies and love. Amen.

✠

O Lord, forgive our sins in the past and those we may commit in the future, but help us to avoid temptation that we may not fall, that we may lead a proper life and make it useful to Thee and our fellow-man. We give Thee thanks for this provision of food from Thy bounty, and pray that Thy mercies may be continued. Amen.

Keep us ever humble, Lord that we may
be the ready recipients of Thy goodness.
Deliver us from pride and wickedness,
and supply our wants. Amen.

O DEAR HEAVENLY FATHER, who lookest
down upon us in mercy and pitying love,
we do thank Thee for our daily repast
from Thine earthly store, for our burden
is light with Thy grace. Amen.

DEAR FATHER, hear the prayer of Thy
children, that as we travel life's journey
from day to day, thanking Thee ever,
Thou wilt lead us on into that Great
Country where our imperfect faith shall
blossom into knowledge, and our feeble
thanks shall give way to the hallelujahs of
Heavenly praise. Amen.

Graces for a New Day

LORD, WE BATHE in the soft light of your
eternal love. But we, created in your image, have assumed the power to destroy
humankind, your creatures, and all that
you have created on this holy earth.
Help us to ensure that the blinding light
of a nuclear holocaust shall never occur.
Help us to ensure that killing radiation
shall not descend through the atmo-
sphere. Help us, God of love, so that our
children and grandchildren, and genera-
tions yet to come, may sit at table and
praise God as we do now, for the food
that they are about to eat. Amen.

DEAR GOD, bless us all with the strength
to withstand the pressures in our daily
lives. Let us look at the demands made
upon us and question their validity. Help
us to understand that with a greater
sense of serenity we can do Thy work
and be joyful. Amen.

CHILDREN come in many colors
They live in different lands
But one God watches over all
We're safe in God's sure hands. Amen.

✠

AS TEENAGERS we come before Thee and
give thanks for the strength and awareness that come each day as we bridge the
difficult journey from childhood to
adulthood. God sustains us in class and
shares our joy. As our minds and bodies
grow may we be ever mindful of the
physical and spiritual nourishment which
God's presence provides. Amen.

✠

LORD, WE humans are the stewards of
your beneficence to our earth. Help us
to act so that the food which you set before us today and in the future may be
free from chemical pollutants. Help us to
ensure that our food shall be free from
radioactive contamination. Help us to
make technology bend to our deepest
needs. Help us, O Lord, to choose life!
Amen.

SO MUCH of the world goes to bed hungry every night, but we are blessed with abundance. The bellies of Third World children swell through malnutrition, but the only way our bellies swell is through overeating. We wonder what God's plan on this earth must be. Help us, O Lord, to an awareness of our spiritual and physical needs, and of the needs of people in all countries of this world—as we give thanks for the food that is set before us. Amen.

✠

LORD, in centuries gone by, the rules were clear and choices were limited. Religious practices were clearly prescribed. People stayed in one village. One's station in life and even occupation were predetermined. Today, our choices in religious belief and practice, who we can marry, where we live, what career we follow, and how we conduct our personal lives are almost limitless. Lord, while we cherish these choices and opportunities, help us to choose wisely and in accordance with Thy divine guidance. Amen.

GOD, you have given us fire and it warmed our hands. From vegetation that grew in your kingdom in ages long past have we extracted fossil fuels. We have made electricity from the force of your surging streams, from the winds of your sighs and from the intensity of your sun's rays. From life's basic atomic structure have we harnessed nuclear energy. Help us, O Lord, to deal wisely with your awesome power we have arrogated to ourselves. Let not nuclear fire destroy all your miracles on this lovely Earth. Amen.

WE GIVE THANKS to God who in six days of creation brought order to our planet and created an environment full of living things. We are grateful for the plant life which gives us our fruits and vegetables and grains. We give thanks for the animals and fowl which provide us with meat and poultry. We reverently accept Thy gifts to us. If we deny ourselves adequate food or a balanced diet, we violate God's plan. Help us, Lord, to eat wisely. Amen.

LORD, help us to remember when it is easy to forget those less fortunate than ourselves. While we sit at this table surrounded by family and friends, others are lost and alone. While we share bread, others go hungry. While we are sheltered from the cold, others are homeless. Lord, help us to remember those less fortunate than ourselves and be thankful. Amen.

I DO NOT love God until I love my neighbor as myself. Help me to bring the blessing of love to others. Let us not be content, O God, when others go hungry, or be serene while some lack their daily bread. Help us to be among those who are willing to sacrifice that others may not hunger, who dare to be bearers of light to the dark loneliness of stricken lives. Let us heed your injunction not to harden our hearts nor shut our hands against the poor. Let our hearts be moved by the misery of others, and dare what must be dared. We are all responsible. Amen.

As we join hands, let us come together, rich and poor, black and white, young and old, enjoying each other's uniqueness. Just as each season brings a new loveliness, so does each man and woman bring forth a special gift, making this world a more beautiful place to live in. Amen.

✠

Lord, we are the children of the age of technology. We rush through our busy days often mindless of the foods we eat and the liquids we drink. In the name of expediency we lose sight of nature's wonderful gifts. Sometimes we do not come to the table as a family to enjoy the harvest of your creation. Lord, help us to be mindful of your gifts. Amen.

✠

Dear Lord, we humans are all made in Thy image. When we at table "break bread," we may be eating rice, or nan, or pita, or noodles, or matzos, or tortillas, or poi, or white bread. We are all God's race and God's color. We are, together, God's family. Amen.